THE MAJOR MENTAL ILLNESSES
VOLUME II

INTRODUCTION

The Axis I psychiatric disorders - schizophrenia, bipolar disorder, and depression – are the focus of hundreds of scholarly papers each year. These articles provide new insights regarding epidemiology, clinical presentation, physical findings, and treatments for these disorders. This guide provides a summary of the latest information available in the professional literature.

Disclaimer:
The author is not on any pharmaceutical advisory boards and does not receive research support from the industry. Every effort has been made to assure there are no errors in this publication, but this guide should not be used as a sole source of information for diagnostic or treatment purposes.

CONTENTS

<u>SCHIZOPHRENIA</u>

The most current view is that schizophrenia is a syndrome rather than a disease, i.e. individuals diagnosed with schizophrenia may have substantial differences in psychopathology, in the same way that individuals with congestive heart failure will have different causes for their condition.

Schizophrenia is associated with marked social and occupational dysfunction and a course of chronic remissions and exacerbations. The three major dimensions of schizophrenia are psychotic symptoms, deficit symptoms and cognitive symptoms.

Demographics

Schizophrenia occurs in ~1% of the population at any given time. There are 20 million cases world-wide, 2-4 million in the U.S. There are 50,000 new cases each year with some pockets worldwide of greater and lower risk. The course of remissions and relapse may differ across cultures. Age of onset is almost always before 35 years old. Intelligence follows a normal bell curve. Slightly more men than women develop schizophrenia (3:2). No racial differences are seen (MacDonald A., Schulz S., 2009).

The Three Aspects of Schizophrenia

1) **Deficit Symptoms** (restricted emotional expression, reduced drive, poor rapport) Deficit symptoms may be the most distinctive feature of schizophrenia. They appear earlier, show more heritability, and are harder to treat. Psychotic symptoms remain relatively stable over time, but negative symptoms worsen. Recent studies suggest that deficit/disorganizational pathology is most strongly associated with early age of onset and male gender, implicating a developmental/genetic cause (Dominguez M., et al., 2010). Antipsychotics can cause negative symptoms in healthy volunteers (Artaloytia J., et al., 2006). Clozapine is the only antipsychotic drug that has any efficacy for deficit symptoms (Ongur D., 2009).

2) **Psychotic Symptoms** (hallucinations, delusions) Auditory hallucinations are experiences of hearing voices or sounds that are generated in the brain, rather than by sound waves. (It is estimated that most adults experience pseudo-hallucinations

(e.g.hearing one's named called). Up to 5% may experience occasional actual hallucinations not due to schizophrenia (Thraenhardt B., 2007)). Delusions are fixed, false beliefs caused by a mental illness. Most frequent are delusions of persecution, as well as being controlled by a force, atomic power, or X-rays from space. Sometimes private language, neologisms, mutism, echolalia, and word salad are seen, as well as excessive concreteness, thought blocking, and thought withdrawal. Psychotic symptoms occur later in development and are associated with environmental risk factors (urbanicity, cannabis exposure, trauma.) It is possible that genetic/*in utero* risks which lead to deficit syndromes may in turn create a vulnerability for developing psychotic symptoms after environmental stresses (Carpenter W., 2010).

3) **Cognitive Symptoms** A normal score on the Wisconsin Card Sorting Test among 10 year olds is 5 out of 6 categories correct. People with schizophrenia who are employed can often get 3 categories correct. Unemployed people with schizophrenia typically get 1 correct. Cognitive symptoms are the primary cause of psychosocial incapacity (Evins A., et al., 2004, MacDonald A., Schulz S., 2009). As mentioned above, these symptoms may be linked to deficit symptoms through some sort of common genetic/*in utero* risk. There are 7 different areas of disruption:
    1) Verbal learning and memory (following instructions)
    2) Speed of processing (moving from one task to another)
    3) Working memory (taking and remembering a phone number)
    4) Reasoning and problem solving (planning a shopping trip)
    5) Attention and vigilance (talking when there are distractions)
    6) Visual learning and memory (remembering pictures, images)
    7) Social learning (recognizing feelings in others)

No antipsychotic restores cognition (Ongur D., 2009).

Gender Issues

There is a higher incidence of schizophrenia among men, with a correspondingly earlier age of diagnosis. Deficit symptoms are more prevalent in men. Men smoke and abuse substances more. They have worse premorbid histories, more negative symptoms, and a poorer course (MacDonald A., Schulz S., 2009).

Therapeutic alliance is stronger in women. Women have more comorbid problems with mood, sleep, pain, allergies, endocrine, eating disorders, personality disorders and psychophysiological disorders. Women have more affective symptoms, auditory hallucinations and persecutory delusions, but experience less severe symptoms, fewer hospitalizations, shorter admissions, more employment, less trouble with the law, and have better intimate relationships. They respond to lower doses of medication. Women tend to have more side effects and tardive dyskinesia (Seeman M., 2004). Mortality is lower in women. Risk of unplanned pregnancy is high due to rape or ineffective birth control.

Genetics

Genetic Risk for Schizophrenia

General population	1%
Second degree relative	5%
Parent	13%
Twin (dizygotic)	17%
2 parents	46%
Twin (monozygotic)	48%

The most significant risk factor for developing schizophrenia is having a first-degree relative. However, most people with schizophrenia do not have an affected relative. Furthermore, studies have shown that while the overall genetic contribution to schizophrenia may be large, the contribution of individual genes is small. Pre and peri-natal complications and exposures have a stronger effect than individual genes (Gilmore J., 2010).

A number of environmental risk factors have been demonstrated:
1) Winter birth (Saran M., et al., 2007)
2) Urban density may account for up to 30% of the risk (Krabbendam L., Os J., 2005)
3) Maternal infection with Toxoplasma gondii (parasite), herpes simplex, Cytomegalovirus. The risk of having a child with

schizophrenia increases 3 times if the mother has flu in the first trimester (Brown A., Derkits E., 2010).
4) Malnutrition during fetal life
5) Extreme prematurity
6) Hypoxia and ischemia that may affect brain volume
7) Level of family functioning (i.e. a healthy environment is protective. There is no evidence that families cause schizophrenia in genetically protected children, but childhood trauma is associated with psychosis.)
8) A small, but significant association with cannabis use (Foti D., et al., 2010, Henquet C., et al., 2005)
9) A puzzling association with a range of autoimmune diseases (Eaton W., et al., 2006)
10) Maternal depression combined with genetic vulnerability to psychosis (Gilmore J., 2010).

In essence, schizophrenia is likely the result of an abnormal developmental trajectory contributed to by the interaction of thousands of genes and multiple environmental risk factors (Gilmore J., 2010).

Brain Studies and Neurochemistry

Brain imaging shows enlargement in the ventricular system and decreases in volume in most of the cortical gray matter regions. There is reduced anterior cingulate volume and white matter abnormalities (Pies R., 2008). Most current hypotheses focus on disturbances of broad systems of interconnected regions, like the frontolimbic or frontostriatal systems. At a molecular level, there is evidence of excessive dopamine transmission in the subcortex (D_2 receptors), and decreased transmission in the cortex (D_1 receptors), which may be accounted for by an abnormality in N-Methyl-D-aspartate (NMDA) transmission (Sabb F., Bilder R., 2006). Specifically, too little glutamate in the cortex may lead to low stimulation of mesolimbic GABA neurons, allowing too much dopamine to be released in the mesolimbic area, leading to positive symptoms. Additionally, glutamate hypoactivity may lead to low excitation of mesocortical dopamine neurons and too little dopamine in the cortex, accounting for cognitive and negative symptoms. There is also great research interest in glial cells, cells in the brain between neurons, and their function in clearing out glutamate and GABA in the synapses between neurons (Ongur D., 2009).

Comorbidities
<u>Uncontrolled Hostility and Violence</u>

While individuals with schizophrenia can become agitated and sometimes hostile under stress, most do not become violent. A recent longitudinal study of 13,800 people with at least two hospitalizations for schizophrenia found a violence conviction rate of 17.1% for men and 5.6% for women. The hazard ratio for risk factors was 3.54 for previous violence, 3.22 for drug abuse, 2.35 for alcohol abuse, and 2.33 for parental violent crime. This suggests the importance of factors other than psychosis as important factors in violence (Fazel S., et al., 2009). It is useful to think of violence in schizophrenia as having two distinct pathways: one associated with premorbid conditions such as family history, gender, childhood trauma, conduct disorder, antisocial behavior; the other pathway associated with the pathology of schizophrenia such as psychosis, agitation, cognitive impairments, etc. Violence is also related to context: substance abuse, unemployment, neighborhood, and poor adherence to treatment (Volavka J., Citrome L., 2011). Command hallucinations increase risk in some patients but not others (McNiel D., et al., 2000).

<u>Anxiety/Depression</u>

40% of people with schizophrenia report suicidal ideation, 25-50% attempt suicide, 10-15% die of suicide. This is 50 times higher than the general population. At high risk are young white males who are depressed, unmarried, unemployed, socially isolated, functionally impaired and lack external support. Those who have been to college may be a higher risk (Palmer B., et al., 2005). Most depressive episodes coincide with psychotic episodes and antipsychotics are the treatment of choice. Often, an antidepressant is not needed, but clients should be regularly evaluated for symptoms of depression, and antidepressants can be used with antipsychotics.

45% of schizophrenic clients have an anxiety disorder. Panic disorder is the most frequent comorbidity, followed by social anxiety, PTSD, and obsessive-compulsive disorder (Evins A., et al., 2004).

<u>Substance abuse</u>

Substance abuse and psychosis commonly appear together, and many people with schizophrenia engage in polysubstance abuse. Substance abuse exacerbates the illness, increases the risk of suicide, victimization and number of hospitalizations. There is a worse prognosis, and worsening of economic status (Buckley P., 2006). On the positive side, clients report using substances helps them cope with symptoms of schizophrenia, alleviates boredom, anxiety, sadness, distress, and gives them an activity to share with friends. The Clinical Antipsychotic Trials for Intervention Effectiveness (CATIE) study showed that compared with abstinence, substance use and substance use disorder (except for cocaine) was associated with higher psychosocial functioning in people with schizophrenia (Swartz M., et al., 2006).

People with schizophrenia have rates of smoking between 74-92%. Smoking induces P450 liver enzymes, and lowers the blood levels of haloperidol, fluphenazine, thiothixene, clozapine and olanzapine. Smoking may be so prevalent because:

1) nicotinic cholinergic receptors may normalize auditory sensory gating in schizophrenic clients
2) concentration is improved
3) nicotinic receptors on dopamine neurons may increase dopamine and decrease EPSE's.
4) smoking may have antidepressant effects (Anthenelli R., 2005).

Treatment of Substance Abuse in a Schizophrenic Population

Treatments designed for individuals with substance use disorders cannot simply be applied to people with schizophrenia. Treaters must face the additional problems of the effect of the thought disorder and other symptoms, problems with motivation, poor self-efficacy, and maladaptive personal skills.

Three organizing principles need to guide treatment (Tenhula W., et al., 2009):

1) Integration of substance abuse and mental health treatment. These individuals are often excluded from traditional substance abuse treatment settings. The complications of navigating different settings, different providers, different insurance benefits are particularly daunting for the client wit schizophrenia. Unfortunately, while there is strong evidence that integration of treatment services work well for dually diagnosed clients, the typical financing and organization of health care systems do not allow this to occur.
2) Harm reduction approaches should be used. Harm reduction approaches place a priority on reducing the risks of substance

abuse, rather than insisting on abstinence as the only goal. Any reduction in the frequency or intensity of substance abuse is a positive change. Research shows that a requirement of abstinence for admittance to a program, or for housing is often too difficult a threshold to achieve. Such requirements exclude too many clients from treatment.

3) Accommodation of cognitive and motivational deficits. Cognitive and social deficits in schizophrenia affect memory, consequential thinking and problem solving. Social impairments include asking for appropriate help and support. Treatment must take into account how these clients differ form the usual participants in substance abuse treatment groups.

Clients need a nonjudgmental, nurturing ally. Clinicians need to recognize:

1) possible stigma against clients with mental illness and on medication in 12-step programs
2) the need to be more active in therapy because of problems with attention, memory and reality awareness
3) the need for patience and persistence
4) the problem of denial of both illnesses and subsequent poor adherence to treatment

One of the keys to success is to ensure that patients have access to residential services and vocational support. Some second-generation antipsychotics may be helpful in reducing substance abuse, but first-generation antipsychotics are not (Green A., et al., 2007).

Natural History of Schizophrenia

Schizophrenia begins with genetic vulnerability. The illness lies dormant until the premorbid phase, which may be entirely asymptomatic or may cause impaired attention, some social deficits, and soft neurologic signs. Next the illness enters the prodromal phase. Nearly 80% of clients with schizophrenia experience a prodrome beginning in puberty that lasts a few months to several years. Common features include anxiety, blunted affect, depression, irritability, loss of initiative, sleep disturbance, social withdrawal, worsening referential and paranoid thinking, cognitive deficits and declining academic functioning. An estimated 30-50% will progress to schizophrenia within a year. (This may be as high as 74-81%

if there is also a family history and other specific variables (*Harvard Mental Health Letter,* Dec. 2009). With the onset of illness, the disease enters the <u>progressive phase</u>. 86% of first episode clients recover after their first episode with treatment (75% to full remission and 11% to partial remission) and 14% remain treatment refractory. The vast majority of clients will relapse in three years. Most of the deterioration in the illness occurs during the first 5 years. The illness then moves into the <u>chronic/residual phase</u> with repeated episodes and relapses. Sufferers often become resistant to medication (Lieberman J., et al., 2006).

The model that best describes the above progression is one that combines a developmental and degenerative focus. Genes probably create a neurodevelopmental and neurodegenerative risk, which in a certain environment, results in the progression seen above (Lieberman J., et al., 2006). However, there is preliminary evidence that cognitive behavior therapy and medication may decrease the risk of progression. Furthermore, one study of 274 clients suggests that a large number of clients with schizophrenia will show periods of recovery and will not experience the severe social isolation that was once described as part of the illness (Harrow M., et al., 2005, Cohen C., et al., 2008). Recovery was also found in a ten-year study of schizophrenic clients with substance use disorders (Drake R., et al., 2006).

Childhood onset schizophrenia does exist, although it is quite rare. Less than 1% of people with schizophrenia have this diagnosis in childhood. Symptoms overlap with autism spectrum and speech and language disorders. The earlier the onset, the poorer the prognosis (Khurana A., et al., 2007).

Prevention of Schizophrenia

Researchers have devoted considerable effort evaluating ways to prevent the progression to schizophrenia from the premorbid or prodromal phase. Early use of antipsychotics has proven to be disappointing. There is some preliminary evidence that cognitive behavior therapy geared toward improving memory, attention, and social skills may be helpful. The early use of antidepressants is inconclusive. Finally, there is evidence that omega-3 dietary supplements may have some preventative effect (*Harvard Mental Health Letter,* Dec. 2009).

Treatment

Treatment needs to be initiated as quickly as possible after the beginning of symptoms, since the duration of untreated psychosis is related to poor outcome (MacDonald A., Schulz S., 2009).

The goals of treatment are defined by the model of treatment. In the maintenance model, relapse prevention is the focus and the emphasis is on higher doses of antipsychotics with a strong emphasis on compliance and risk reduction. Success is measured by the number of psychotic relapses. In the remission model, the goal is to treat to the point where there are no longer any psychotic symptoms. Medications are the primary modality and success is measured by symptom scales. In the recovery model, the goal is to help people live and participate fully in their communities. Specific goals are set by the client. Success is measured by client satisfaction and community measures. Evidence is accumulating that the recovery model is a realistic approach (Harrow M., et al., 2005, Cohen C., et al., 2008, Drake R., et al., 2006).

In surveys, clients with schizophrenia identify depression/anxiety, Parkinsonian side effects from medication, and not wanting to take medication as the factors that most interfere with the quality of their lives. Employment enhances quality of life. These should be important targets for intervention (Hofer A., et al., 2004).

A large, non-industry sponsored medication research trial is the Clinical Antipsychotic Trials for Interventions Effectiveness (CATIE). This study, sponsored by NIMH, has had two published phases. Altogether, 1,493 patients began the study. The results confirm that a significant number of clients discontinue their antipsychotic treatment because of side effects and lack of efficacy (74%). There may be some small, but clinically significant differences in efficacy and tolerability among the second-generation antipsychotics. Clozapine is the most effective drug for those who fail to respond adequately to initial treatment, but has serious side effects. Among the other drugs, the fact that there is little difference in efficacy (confirmed by more recent studies) suggests that if a patient is doing "well enough," don't switch drugs to find a better one. If the patient is having trouble with side effects, do consider another drug, since side effects do vary (Lieberman J., Stroup T., 2011).

Antipsychotic drugs are effective for psychosis, but are not "anti-schizophrenic." Efficacy for negative symptoms and cognitive impairments is modest at best (Green M., 2007). The benefit of maintenance drug treatment is primarily relapse prevention, not comprehensive treatment.

Some data that suggest antipsychotic medications may have a neuroprotective effect in schizophrenia if they are given early enough in the illness. Research is ongoing (Lieberman J., et al., 2006).

Psychosocial Treatments

There is a 40% relapse rate even in medication compliant clients, so medication should not be the sole treatment for this condition. Research shows the following interventions are effective:

Assertive Community Treatment: reduces the frequency of hospitalization, increases housing stability, and shows high satisfaction on ratings from clients and families. It has not been shown to be superior to standard care on measures of mental state and social functioning. It does not result in cost savings except for populations that are already high users of inpatient care (Clark R., Samnaliev M., 2005). (Case management alone is not the same as ACT and does not have clinically significant results.)

Integrated Dual Disorders Treatment Supported Employment: the individual placement and support (IPS) model is effective in maintaining competitive employment (Clark R., Samnaliev M., et al., 2005).

Family Intervention: reduces relapse, improves symptomatic recovery, and enhances family outcomes. Programs must last longer than 6 months (Kuipers E., 2007).

Social Skills Training: improves social skills.

Personal Therapy: improves psychosocial functioning (Dickerson F., et al., 2006)

Akathisia is one of the most important variables that determines whether clients choose to stay in psychosocial treatment.

Cognitive-Behavioral Therapy

Two randomized controlled trials have demonstrated that patients with schizophrenia who receive cognitive-behavioral therapy along with medication show improvement in depressive and positive and negative symptoms, although the studies were contradictory as to whether these were short or long-term gains. Results are also contradictory concerning relapse, rehospitalization, and social functioning (Dickerson F., et al., 2006, Turkington D., et al., 2006).

Key techniques of cognitive therapy include:
1) developing a therapeutic alliance
2) developing an explanation of the client's symptoms that is satisfactory to both the client and the clinician
3) reducing the stress and severity of positive symptoms by normalization, exploration and building strategies of adaptation

Vocational Needs

Among clients treated with first-generation antipsychotics, only 10% ever work fulltime and 33% work at supported employment. Working at a paid job is one of the most important determinants of quality of life. Cognitive dysfunction is the most important variable in being able to work.

The CATIE Project collected data on employment and functioning of 1,400 clients. 14.5% of clients reported participating in competitive employment, 12.6% reported other employment, and 72.6% reported no employment. Employment was associated with:

- Less severe negative and positive symptoms
- Better cognitive function
- Psychological characteristics of motivation, empathy
- Higher education
- Availability of psychosocial rehabilitation

African-Americans and those receiving disability payments were less likely to be competitively employed, i.e. the differences between being competitively employed and having supported employment seem to be primarily social (Rosenheck R., et al., 2006).

The cognitive mechanisms that cause the actual functional disability in schizophrenia appear to be those that affect making social inferences (Sergi M., et al., 2006). Patients with schizophrenia have difficulty in correctly identifying emotions in others (Schneider F., et al., 2006). Consequently, clients will have problems with:

- interpreting the behaviors of co-workers (playful or threatening)
- understanding how personal work relationships should be recognizing how their behavior affects others
- job-related living supports such as transportation and clothing
- performance of job tasks

Health Problems

Mortality of clients with schizophrenia is 1.6-2.6x greater than in people without schizophrenia. Medical and surgical hospitalizations for people with schizophrenia have twice the odds of adverse events than those without (Daumit G., et al., 2006). Life expectancy is 20% shorter (61 versus 76). This differential mortality gap has worsened in recent decades (Saha S., et al., 2007).

The major cause of premature death is cardiovascular. In human beings, cardiovascular risk is additive with the following:

- Body Mass Index (BMI) >27
- Total cholesterol >220
- Hypertension
- Diabetes
- Smoking

People with schizophrenia are at higher risk for all of these.

The "metabolic syndrome" increases the risk for cardiovascular events above and beyond the risks of these individual factors. Metabolic syndrome consists of three or more of the following:

- Abdominal obesity (waistline men >40, women >35
- Triglycerides >=150
- HDL men <40, women <50
- Blood pressure >=130/85
- Fasting glucose >=110

Clients who have schizophrenia and bipolar disorder, as well as people who take certain second-generation antipsychotics are at increased risk for metabolic syndrome (Meyer J., et al., 2007).

Specific Issues With Health (Marder S., 2004)

<u>Weight gain and obesity</u>

Patients with schizophrenia are more likely to be overweight than the general population (42% vs. 27%). Clients on antipsychotics frequently experience a weight gain of 7-10%. Clozapine and olanzapine cause the most significant increase. Weight gain caused by medications is not dose related. Health recommendations are:

1) Monitor body mass index (BMI) for all patients.
2) Weigh patient at each visit for six months when starting new medication
3) Weight gain of 1 BMI (~6 pounds) indicates medication change

Diabetes

Clients with schizophrenia have twice the incidence of diabetes. Some antipsychotics are associated with the onset of diabetes. Health recommendations include:

1) Baseline glucose for all patients starting on a new antipsychotic
2) Clients with significant risk for diabetes (family history, BMI>24, waist >34 for women, >39 for men) should have fasting glucose or HbA1c every four months then yearly
3) Clients should know symptoms of new onset diabetes (weight change, polyuria, polydipsia)

Hyperlipidemia

Clients with chronic psychiatric disorders have a higher incidence of hyperlipidemia. Clozapine and olanzapine worsen lipid profiles. Health recommendations:

1) Monitor lipids
2) Clients with metabolic syndrome should be monitored by a primary health care provider

QT prolongation

Certain antipsychotics can be associated with ECG abnormalities that may indicate a risk of potential fatal arrhythmias.

1) Clients with known heart disease, history of syncope, family history of sudden death at an early age, or congenital long QT syndrome should not be prescribed thioridazine, Mesoridazine, or pimozide
2) If ziprasidone is prescribed, these clients should have a baseline ECG and follow-up ECG if symptoms occur

Cardiac arrhythmia and risk of death in older adults

A "black box warning" from the FDA notes a doubling risk of death in patients with dementia who are treated with atypical antipsychotics. More recent reviews have found that both typical and atypical antipsychotics cause an increased risk of cardiac death at any age (Ray W., et al., 2009). Getting baseline and follow-up ECG's may be prudent for at risk patients who are taking any antipsychotic.

<u>Elevated prolactin</u>

Certain antipsychotics are associated with increases in prolactin. The health effects of this increase are variable.

- Ask female clients about changes in menstruation, libido, and lactation
- Ask men about libido, erectile and ejaculatory dysfunction
- Prolactin levels should be taken if indicated

<u>EPS, akathisia, tardive dyskinesia</u>

Second-generation antipsychotics reduce the risk of tardive dyskinesia.

1) Clients should be examined for movement disorders before starting antipsychotic medication and should be monitored for two weeks after starting.
2) Clients should be examined every six months if they are on a first-generation antipsychotic and yearly if they are on a second-generation.

<u>MAJOR DEPRESSION</u>

Depression is a mood (experienced by everyone) and a medical syndrome (a cluster of symptoms, only one of which is mood). In clinical practice, the diagnosis of "depression" is used in a wide variety of different disorders, including major depressive disorder, bipolar disorder, dysthymia, bereavement and bipolar disorder. People with a major depressive episode tend to withdraw and are able to express a limited range of emotions. They are often obsessively focused on themselves and how they feel. In the primary care setting, the following often indicate depression: sleep disturbance, fatigue and multiple somatic complaints.

Symptoms of Depression
Affective
       depressed mood
Vegetative
       weight loss, weight gain, or change in appetite
       insomnia or hypersomnia
       decreased sex drive

Behavioral

> psychomotor retardation or agitation nearly every day
> fatigue
> diminished interest or pleasure in almost all activities

Cognitive

> feelings of worthlessness or guilt
> diminished ability to think and concentrate
> poor frustration tolerance
> negative distortions

Impulse Control

> recurrent thoughts of death or suicide, homicide

Somatic

> headaches, stomachaches, muscle tension, pain

The overlap of depression and pain is particularly apparent in syndromes such as fibromyalgia, irritable bowel syndrome, low back pain, headaches, and nerve pain. About 65% of people seeking help for depression report at least one type of pain syndrome. Researchers have found that pain, depression and anxiety share both neuroanatomy (somatosensory cortex, amygdala, hypothalamus, and anterior cingulated gyrus) and two neurotransmitters (serotonin and norepinephrine) (*Harvard Mental Health Letter,* May 2010).

Clients with depression have difficulties in interpersonal relationships, largely related to problems with emotional perception and executive function (memory, attention.) People suffering from acute episodes of depression have a diminished ability to distinguish facial emotional expression. They have problems misidentifying happy facial expressions as sad (Fu C., et al., 2007). There is impaired ability to perceive black and white contrast. The world really does look gray! (*Harvard Mental Health Letter,* Nov. 2010). In addition, there is evidence of mood state-dependent learning. Clients don't remember ever feeling good, possibly increasing the risk of suicide. These memories can be retrieved with proper prompting and cueing.

Depression in Borderline Personality Disorder

The dysphoria or depression that is seen in borderline personality is usually experienced in the context of interpersonal relationships. The mood shifts, hour by hour, and includes feelings of emptiness, loneliness, fears of abandonment, and self-condemnation. There are frequent low injury suicide attempts.

Antidepressants do not ameliorate these feelings and behaviors. If vegetative symptoms are present, indicating a major depressive episode, antidepressants can be useful in relieving them (Paris J., 2010, Silk K., 2010).

Demographics

Depression is one of the most common psychiatric disorders. According to NESARC, the 12-month prevalence of depression is 5.28% and lifetime prevalence is 13.23%. Those at high risk for depression include Native Americans (19.17%) and whites (14.58%). African Americans (8.93%), Hispanics (9.64%), and Asians (8.77%) are at lower risk. There is high comorbidity for anxiety disorders (36%), especially generalized anxiety disorder and a personality disorder (37%) (Hasin D., et al., 2005).

Mortality from depression is high. 45.5% of depressed clients report they want to die, 36.4% have considered suicide, and 8.8% report a suicide attempt (Hasin D., et al., 2005). Risk of completed suicide is 20x that of the general population, a 14.6% lifetime risk. 30-70% of suicides have a depressive disorder (Baldessarini R., 2003). 20% of clients experience depression after a myocardial infarction, and have a 2.5 greater risk of mortality. Responding to treatment with antidepressants lowers this risk, and non-responders to antidepressants have the highest risk for new cardiac events in the next 2.5 years, regardless of their cardiac impairment (de Jonge P., et al., 2007, Carney R., Freedland K., 2009). This risk seems to be specifically related to depression that first appears a month after the initial heart attack (Parker G., et al., 2008).

Depression in Children and Adolescents

Until the 1980's, it was not thought that young people could become depressed. It is now known that depression effects up to 2.5% of children and 8.3% of adolescents (Singh M., et al., 2007). Among preschoolers, anhedonia is the most specific symptom of depression, accompanied frequently by sadness, social withdrawal, excessive guilt, extreme fatigue, diminished cognitive abilities and irritability (Luby J., 2004). Irritability, in fact, is the most common presentation of many mental health problems in children, including depression, but is not a good proxy for feelings of sadness in preschool children, as has previously been thought. Caregivers may fail to report symptoms, or may unwittingly accommodate to them, complicating the diagnosis. There is little empirical basis for treatment, but antidepressants should not be used as first or even second-line treatments in preschool children. Family therapy is the recommended approach, with an emphasis on emotion development. In older school-age children, fluoxetine is the only approved antidepressant (Luby J., 2009).

By adolescence, depression rates have started to climb, and young people are more able to describe themselves as depressed. The three strongest risk factors for adolescent depression are 1) parental depression 2) symptoms of depression but not yet a full-blown episode 3) prior depression. Risk may be reduced by participating in sports and going to bed by 10 p.m. (*Harvard Mental Health Letter,* May 2010). Substance abuse has a bidirectional relationship with depression in adolescents, both leading to depression and resulting from depression (Hallfors D., et al., 2005). Other nonspecific risk factors include poverty, exposure to violence and abuse, social isolation and family breakup. Other protective factors include the presence of supportive adults, strong family relationships, strong peer relationships and coping skills (Gladstone T., et al., 2010).

Suicidality first arises as a public health problem in adolescence. The use of certain antidepressants seems to increase the risk of suicidal thinking and behavior, but not increase mortality among teens, so they should not be withheld from young people who need them (Singh M., et al., 2007). The unfortunate result of these warnings has been a decrease in prescriptions of antidepressants for those who need them (Emslie G., 2008).

Three non-industry funded studies have looked at depression treatment in adolescents (Treatment Resistant Depression in Adolescents TORDIA, Treatment for Adolescents with Depression Study TADS, Adolescent Depression Antidepressant and Psychotherapy Trial ADAPT.) The results suggest that teens are a very responsive treatment group, with 60-70% getting better with medication alone or medication plus CBT. Of those who fail the first antidepressant, 40% will respond to a second. Finally, there is no evidence that CBT alone or as an adjunct is useful in severe depression (Walkup J., 2010).

Psychosocial interventions are also an effective treatment approach for depression in teens. Effective interventions include increasing teen competence in at least one self-identified area, psychoeducation about depression and treatment, teaching self-monitoring skills, cognitive restructuring and behavioral activation (Parry P., 2010).

Depression in the Older Adults

There is no increase in depression for those elderly people living in the community. However, all medical illnesses increase the rate of depression. Rates of depression among older people are as follows (*Harvard Mental Health Letter*, Feb 2008):

- Community: 1-5%
- Hospitalized: 12%
- Requiring assistance at home: 15%
- Nursing home: 29-52%
- Being treated for a serious illness: 39-47%

Older clients do not complain of depression to their doctors because that is not why they come to the doctor. They complain of low energy, poor appetite, poor sleep, and various somatic complaints like heart palpitations, tremors, and shortness of breath. Certain illnesses and drugs may mimic symptoms of depression, including hypothyroidism, B vitamin deficiencies, blood pressure medicine, etc. (*Harvard Mental Health Letter*, Feb 2008).

Mild cognitive impairment in depression ranges from 25-50% and may persist for up to a year after an episode. Deficits include slowed information processing, poor attention and concentration, difficulty with memory and executive functions. Later onset depression (60 years or older) is more frequently characterized by greater apathy, greater cardiovascular morbidity, and a stronger association with dementia. It seems that depression is a risk factor for dementia in some individuals, while it is an early sign of dementia for others (Potter G., Steffens D., 2007). Older people with symptoms of depression should always have a good cardiovascular assessment, as well as an assessment of their cognitive status.

Distinguishing the cognitive impairments of depression from dementia is an important clinical skill. Decline in mental functioning is more rapid with depression than dementia. People with depression are less often disoriented. Concentration is more a problem with depression and short-term memory more a problem with dementia. Writing, speaking, and motor skills are not usually impaired in depression (*Harvard Mental Health Letter,* Feb. 2008).

In addition to increasing morbidity and mortality from various medical conditions, depression is a strong risk factor for suicide. Older white and Native-American men have the highest suicide rate in the U.S. general population.

Bereavement

Bereavement is a universal experience related to the loss of a loved one. It can be thought of as an attachment trauma. The psychological reaction to bereavement is grief. Grief is not a single emotion, but a combination of different emotions, including the negative feelings of sadness, anxiety, guilt, anger and shame; and the positive emotions of happy reminiscence, pride in the deceased, warmth and relief.

Acute grief lasts most of the day, every day for up to six months, and then recurs transiently. It is characterized by a sense of disbelief, dominant painful emotions, preoccupation with thoughts of the deceased, and attenuation of interest and engagement with ongoing life. This painful state normally transitions into "integrated grief," which can be thought of as a permanent background state, where positive emotions, such as acceptance, forgiveness and compassion predominate. There is no evidence that most people go through a linear, five step process as famously described by Dr. Kubler-Ross. Rather, people seem to undergo several prolonged and overlapping phases. There are a number of different and useful conceptualizations of this process (*Harvard Mental Health Letter,* Dec. 2011).

Rarely, grief may be complicated – great difficulty accepting death, excessively painful memories which may be very difficult to access or very intrusive, overwhelming feelings of guilt or yearning. Complicated grief is not limited to those people who had ambivalent relationships with the deceased. It is seen just as frequently in those with very positive and close relationships. Complicated grief is usually not diagnosed until more than six months after the death. Complicated grief is associated with bad health outcomes, including cancer diagnosis, high blood pressure, cardiac problems, and suicide (Hensley P., 2006).

Although grief may look like depression, there are some important differences. The symptoms of depression tend to be pervasive, as opposed to grief where the symptoms are more episodic. Depression is more likely to show the following: apathy, suicidality, pervasive guilty ruminations, and poor self-esteem. Grief is more likely to show yearning, preoccupation with the loved one, crying, disbelief, and the retained ability to experience positive emotions. Symptoms of PTSD are more likely to have symptoms of hyperarousal, scanning for threat, avoidance, be associated with a traumatic death (Gray M., et al., 2006).

In children the course of grief is determined by who else is important in the child's life. This is not an important feature in grief progression in adults. Children don't usually develop complicated grief unless they are afraid of their own death.

There is some controversy about treating the symptoms associated with grief. Approximately 40% of the bereaved meet criteria for a major depressive episode a month after the loss, 15% at one year post-loss. This appears to have a 1:1 gender distribution, unlike major depressive disorder. Studies indicate that symptoms of depression are helped by antidepressant treatment, but symptoms of grief are not (Hensly P., 2006). Since in almost every case, bereavement resolves on its own in about 6 months, the overwhelming consensus is to let grief take its course as part of the range of normal human experience, *as long as the symptoms are manageable and the individual is not suffering from a major depressive episode.* This is supported by the observation that virtually all people suffering from bereavement regard their reactions as normal. It must be kept in mind, however, that severe symptoms in the first six months, or the presence of depression, predict a poor outcome, and should be treated (Shear K., 2009).

Complicated grief does not seem to respond to medication, and probably requires specialized therapy. Such therapy involves both grieving the loss and restoring life functioning (Shear K., 2005).

Gender Issues

Women are twice as likely to suffer from depression as men. The separation emerges during a short time span (5 years) that is coincident with the onset of puberty. Social and hormonal influences contribute to making adolescence a difficult transition for girls (Seeman M., 2006). Additionally, menopause is strongly associated with new onset depression (Cohen L., et al., 2006).

Women are more likely than men to describe themselves as depressed. They have more depressive symptoms and a higher degree of distress, and more seasonal affective disorder. They more commonly present with the "atypical" symptoms of depression: hypersomnia, psychomotor retardation, worthlessness, guilt, anxiety and somatization. Women attempt suicide 3 times as often as men. They are more likely to have comorbid anxiety and eating disorders (Sloan D., Kornstein S., 2003).

College education and being in a first marriage confers a lower risk of depression for women. If a woman hasn't been to college, she does better if she works outside the home. Single mothers have twice the risk of depression as married mothers (Sloan D., Kornstein S., 2003).

Emotionally supportive relationships are substantially more protective against major depression for women than men (Kendler K., et al., 2005). Women's friendship networks are larger, and this theoretically serves as both a buffer and risk for exposure to stress. Family ties are perceived differently between men and women, with marriage protecting men from mental illness, but creating more of a risk to mental health for women. Presumable this is due to the burden of the caretaking role women usually assume (Seeman M., 2006).

For men, the most likely reason to seek help is a feeling of failing to meet expectations. The precipitant is likely to be work problems or divorce/separation. Men also complain of difficulty adjusting to major life changes, increasing self-doubts, and feeling overwhelmed by the needs of others. Their symptoms are likely to be social isolation, substance abuse, irritability and risk taking. Men are more likely to have substance abuse problems (Sloan D., Kornstein S 2003).

<u>Pregnancy</u>

Recent studies indicate 10% of women have depressive symptoms during pregnancy. Women with a previous major depression are most at risk. Discontinuation of antidepressants is associated with high rates of relapse, although the risk of suicide is low during pregnancy. Maternal depression is linked to poor neonatal outcome including preterm birth, lower birth weight, smaller head and lower APGAR scores. (Nonacs R., Coen L., 2003).

Antidepressant medications diffuse readily across the placenta. No psychotropic drug has been approved by the FDA for use during pregnancy. Antidepressants carry a small risk for birth defects. More likely is the 30% chance that a neonate will experience an abstinence syndrome of lack of crying, increased muscle tone, irritability, abnormal breathing, and disrupted sleep within 48 hours after birth if exposed to antidepressants in the third trimester. These symptoms are mild and self-limiting (Pies R., 2006). There is also evidence that antidepressants during pregnancy may increase the risk of pre-term birth (Suri R., et al., 2007).

<u>Postpartum Depression</u>

Postpartum depression is the most common complication of childbirth in the U.S. In the first 48 hours after birth, the mother's levels of estrogen and progesterone drop suddenly by a factor of 50 (Gaschler K., 2008). Postpartum "baby blues" are fairly common and effect up to 75% of women. These typically resolve within a week or two. 13% of women will develop post-partum depression. (The prevalence of depression in childbearing age women is 12%.) Risk factors for PPD are a history of depression in the woman or her family, poor intimate relationships, inadequate social support, stressful life events and child-care related stressors. The most significant impact of the depression are the effects on the baby, which include behavioral problems, delayed cognitive and linguistic development, and higher risk for future psychiatric problems (Flynn H., 2005, Johnson P., Flake E., 2007).

0.1% of women will develop a post-partum psychosis, which is a medical emergency and can lead to the mother hurting her child. Onset is usually within two weeks of delivery. The risk seems to be highest in women with a history of bipolar disorder (Flynn H., 2005). See <u>www.womensmentalhealth.org</u> for current information about women and mood disorders (website run by Massachusetts General Hospital). See also <u>www.toxnet.nlm.nih.gov</u> and <u>www.postpartum.net</u>.

Seasonal Affective Disorder

Seasonal affective disorder (SAD) is one of the few psychiatric conditions with a predictable time of onset and remission. As originally defined, it is a syndrome in which depression develops during autumn or winter and remits in the spring or summer. This tendency to experience seasonal mood changes is quite common and ranges from the mild to the subsyndromal, to the extreme.

Many patients develop so-called atypical depressive symptoms, including increased duration of sleep, increased appetite, weight gain and carbohydrate craving. Patients tend to have less suicidal ideation and less morning worsening of symptoms. Children will often present with fatigue, irritability, sleep inertia, and school problems.

The most interesting facet of the disorder is the response to light. 94% of patients report that travel nearer to the equator during the winter months markedly decreases their symptoms. Exposure to bright light is the treatment of choice. The illness occurs more frequently in women than men, and in younger individuals. Some patients remit as they get older, others retain their seasonal pattern throughout their life (Magnusson A., Partonen T., 2005).

Evidence is strong that bright light therapy works for those patients with a seasonal pattern. It is not so strong as an adjunctive therapy for depression without a seasonal component. Most recommendations are for an exposure of 10,000 lux for 20-30 minutes a day. The less bright the light, and the smaller the light box, the more exposure that's needed. The light must shine in the patient's eyes. Morning exposure is best, especially for "morning people" (Carlat D., 2006). Side effects are uncommon. Hypomania is a rare, but possible side effect (Terman M., Terman J., 2005).

Genetics

Family history increases the risk of depression by 1.5 to 3 times. Like most things in mental health, though, the picture is complicated. It appears that the role of genes in this parent to child transmission of depression is relatively small – less than 40%. Genes that influence the development of childhood depression appear to be different than genes that cause depression later on. There are apparently genes that affect the risk of depression differently in men and women. These genes may be hormone specific. The inheritability of major depression is higher in women (42%) than men (29%) (Kendler K., et al., 2006, Reiss D., 2008).

The fact that identical twins show significant differences in incidence of depression, the slow progress in identifying candidate genes, and female predominance have all suggested that "epigenetic" factors may play an important role in depression. In rats, low levels of maternal nurturance lead to increased methylation (repression) of genes in certain areas of the brain (Krishnan V., Nestler E., 2010). Various epigenetic changes have been linked to vulnerability to stress and depressive behaviors.

In humans, parental depression decreases warmth of interaction and increases negativity in the parent-child bond and thereby increases child pathology. But it is also observed that temperament (genes) in children influences parental warmth and negativity. So we are looking at a multifactorial influence of depression genetics, epigenetics, parenting styles, and temperament genes in the child. Fetal exposure to toxins and stress in the mother almost certainly also plays a role (Reiss D., 2008).

In a recent, large adoption study, it was found that maternal, but not paternal, depression was a risk for the development of depression in both biological and adopted adolescents living in the home, continuing the line of evidence that familial transmission of depression results from the environment, not simply the genes (Tully E., et al., 2008).

Environmental Contributors to Depression

The primary environmental predictors for the onset of depression are:
- Stressful life events in the past year
- Genetic factors
- Previous history of major depression
- Neuroticism (Jang 2005).

There is compelling evidence that early life stress such as childhood neglect, physical or sexual abuse, and early parental loss constitutes a major risk factor for depression. In one large prospective longitudinal study, child abuse and neglect were clearly correlated with risk of major depressive disorder in adulthood (Widom C., et al., 2007).

Biological Basis of Depression

The combination of genetics, early life stress, and ongoing life stress may determine individual vulnerability. Stress and glucocorticoids directly lead to cell death and reduce cell resilience by making them more vulnerable to other toxicities, like hypoxia, and hypoglycemia. These changes also decrease the brain's ability to create new neurons. (Gillespie C., Nemeroff C., 2005). Is this the cause of depression?

The observation that 50% of depressed patients improve when treated by agents that increase norepinephrine and serotonin neurotransmission has lead to a hypothesis that deficits in monoamine function are the fundamental "lesion" in depressive illness. There is little primary evidence that this is true (Krishnan V., Nestler E., 2010).

With improvements in neuroimaging techniques, several "network models" of major depression have been described. Defined by dysfunctional interactions among different brain regions (cingulate, paralimbic, subcortical, frontal) when stressed, these models may lead to new treatments, including deep brain stimulation (Mayberg S., 2006, Krishnan V., Nestler E., 2010).

Other lines of investigation include neurogenesis and cell death, the dopamine reward pathways, and the effect of sex hormones, cortisol, and metabolic peptides (Krishnan V., Nestler E., 2010). Finally, over the last two decades evidence has accumulated that people who are depressed often show signs of inflammation with no known underlying disease. Certain cancers, as well as obesity, also linked to depression, increase the release of inflammatory factors in the blood (Shelton R., 2012).

Medical Causes of Depression

Medications - antihypertensives, sedatives, hormones, cimetidine, L-
    dopa
Neurological disorders - stroke, subdural hematoma, multiple sclerosis,
    brain tumors, Parkinson's, Huntington's, seizure disorders,
    syphilis, dementia
Metabolic - hypothyroidism, hyperthyroidism, Cushing's disease,
    pellagra, hypercalcemia, hyponatremia, diabetes, B12 deficiency
Other - pancreatic cancer, viral infections (especially mononucleosis)

Comorbidity With Substance Abuse

Among those with a history of depression, 40.3% have an alcohol use disorder, 17.2% have a drug use disorder, and 30% have nicotine dependence (Hasin D., et al., 2005). Among those with alcohol abuse disorders, 32.75% have a major depression. Among drug abusers, 44.26% have depression (NCS-R).

Individuals with substance abuse often present in a primary care setting with complaints of anxiety, sleep disturbance and depression. Withdrawal from stimulants, especially cocaine causes anhedonia, apathy, depressed mood and possibly suicidal ideation. Chronic use of CNS depressants like alcohol, benzodiazepines, barbiturates and opiates is associated with depressed mood, poor concentration, anhedonia and insomnia. People with late stage alcoholism feel worthless and helpless, have decreased sense of pleasure, sleep disruption, decreased libido and feel depressed. If the depression is treated, abstinence is more successful with less risk of relapse (Geppert C., et al., 2004).

Natural History and Treatment of Depression

The onset of depression usually occurs from 20-40 years old. Most people do not seek help for their depression, even if it is severe (CDC, Sept. 2008). Depression is a lifelong illness, with people likely to relapse within several months of the first episode, especially if antidepressants are discontinued. It is clear from relapse and symptom data that subsyndromal symptoms represent a continuation of the illness and mean that more treatment is necessary (similar to treating an infection.) It is important to treat residual symptoms of depression because they represent a continuation of the disease (Van Rhoads R., Gelenberg A., 2005).

Untreated, an episode of depression will last 6 to 24 months or longer (5-10% have episodes continue for more than two years). The risk of recurrence is 50% after one episode, 70% after two episodes, and 90% after three episodes. People with frequently recurring depression and early age of onset (teens) may suffer from bipolar disorder (*DSM-IV-TR®*). Antidepressant treatment without a mood stabilizer will make them worse.

Psychotherapy

Many kinds of psychotherapy have proven as efficacious for the treatment of depression as medication, and may be better at preventing relapse. Recent review suggests that even the severity of depression does not predict a better response to medication than to psychotherapy (Simon G., Perlis R., 2010), although standard practice would be to treat the most severe depressions with medications. The kind of therapy seems to be less important than other variables, such as treatment alliance, skill of the therapist, belief in the therapy, etc. Cognitive behavioral therapy plus medication may have a synergistic effect, i.e. they work better together than each alone (Hollon et al., 2002). A recent large meta-analysis confirms a small, but statistically significant advantage to using therapy with medication, including better treatment adherence (Cuijpers P., et al., 2009).

Treatment Response to Medication

A seven-year NIMH funded study of 4,041 depressed subjects, Sequences Alternatives to Relieve Depression (STAR*D), found that 33% of patients with depression achieve remission on their first antidepressant (Trivedi M., et al., 2006). Switching to a different antidepressant can improve remission to 50-66% (Quitkin F., 2005, Carlat D., 2007). Achieving remission in symptoms is important because patients who fail to achieve remission:
- Relapse 3 times faster
- Continue to have social and work impairments
- Are at increased risk for substance abuse and suicide

- May develop treatment resistance

Reviews in the *New England Journal of Medicine* (Kirsch et al., 2008) and the *Journal of the American Medical Association* (Fournier et al., 2010) have seriously questioned the efficacy of antidepressants compared to alternative treatments. The conclusion seems to be that antidepressants are as effective, but no more effective than psychotherapy, exercise, stress relief/meditation, and often, placebo. However, standard clinical practice would be to use antidepressants as first line treatment for the most severe depressions.

In terms of how to begin treatment, research to date does not identify any biologic or genetic predictors (e.g. previous response or family response in the past) of sufficient usefulness to guide the choice of medication or psychotherapy, which medication, or which psychotherapy (Simon G., Perlis R., 2010). Discussing potential side effects of the different drug choices with the patient is a good way to begin the selection process.

Treatment Resistant Depression

Approximately 33% of people with depression fail to respond to multiple treatments. Making sure the patient has been tried long enough (12 weeks) on an effective dose of an antidepressant with *no active substance abuse* is a necessary first step. There are no guidelines for which antidepressant to try after the first one has failed, but a second should be tried (Carlat D., 2007). After this, several different augmentation and treatment strategies have been explored (Holzheimer P., Mayberg H., 2010, *Harvard Mental Health Letter,* Dec. 2010):

Augmentation with second-generation antipsychotics – modestly effective but problematic side effects cause adherence problems

Augmentation with T3 hormone or lithium – 25% response rate with either but significant side effects and ongoing blood monitoring for lithium

Augmentation with omega-3 fatty acids - weak, but positive evidence

Augmentation with SAMe – weak but positive evidence, expensive

Augmentation with folic acid – weak evidence, females more responsive

Electroconvulsive Therapy (ECT) – remission rates of 50-60% but high relapse rate

Repetitive Transmagnetic Stimulation (rTMS) – very low response rates, maintenance data unknown, expensive

Vagus Nerve Stimulation (VNS) – does not separate well from placebo and has a high relapse rate, expensive

Deep Brain Stimulation – promising but little data, requires neurosurgery

Other Treatments
Aerobic exercise - 30 minutes/day
Light therapy – generally useful only for seasonal affective disorder
Sleep deprivation - works temporarily, second half of the night
      deprivation is as effective as whole night
Psychosurgery - no controlled studies, a very last resort

Free depression outcome scale:
Patient Health Questionnaire-9 (PHQ-9)
www.depression-primarycare.org/forms/phq_9/

<u>BIPOLAR DISORDER</u>
Bipolar disorder has received an enormous amount of attention over the last 10 years. Whereas the illness used to be considered primarily a disorder of mood swings, it is now thought of as a lifelong illness that creates a vulnerability to depressive and manic episodes and related problems. The nature of this illness is not well understood, but it includes not just episodic mania and depression, but also problems with arousal and catecholaminergic physiology, motivation, impulsivity, and behavioral sensitization in which stressors and substance abuse lead to increased frequency and severity of episodes over time (Swann A., Goldberg J., 2007).

Demographics
Approximately 2.3 million Americans suffer from bipolar disorder. According to NCS-R, the lifetime prevalence of bipolar disorder is 5.1%. The NESARC survey indicates a lifetime prevalence of bipolar I disorder of 3.3%. Native Americans have the highest incidence. Asians and Hispanics have the lowest.

There is ongoing disagreement as to whether bipolar disorder is overdiagnosed or underdiagnosed.

According to the World Health Organization (1990), bipolar disorder is the sixth leading cause of disability worldwide among people 15-44 years old. There is an enormous economic and social impact from this illness (Kessler et al., 2006). Suicide is a significant risk in bipolar disorder, the highest of any psychiatric disorder at 20% (NIMH 2000). As many as 25-50% of clients will make a suicide attempt (Jamison 2000). Most suicidal ideation occurs during depressed or mixed episodes. Suicidal ideation is also highly associated with comorbid substance abuse.

Features/Subtypes

Bipolar disorder is classified according to the severity of the manic state, with bipolar I having full blown mania, bipolar II and cyclothymia having hypomania. Cyclothymia also has milder depressions. Bipolar II does not represent a "milder" illness than bipolar I. Bipolar II is often accompanied by more severe depressions, more chronicity, and more suicidal behavior than bipolar I (Swann A., Goldberg J., 2007).

	Bipolar I	Bipolar II
Psychomotor	retarded	agitated or retarded
Sleep	hypersomnia	insomnia/hypersomnia
Suicide	+++	++++
Switching to	mania	hypomania
Gender	m = f	f > m
Prevalence	1%	1-2.5%

There is often confusion between bipolar disorder and borderline personality disorder because of the frequent mood shifts seen in the latter. Clinicians rarely have difficulty distinguishing a bipolar I manic episode from borderline mood instability but there is a problem with the differential diagnosis between borderline and bipolar II. It is worth noting that the mood "swings" of borderline clients are usually from depression to anger, almost always precipitated by interpersonal stressors. Mood shifts in bipolar II are usually internally driven and the swing is from depression to euphoria or happiness (Paris J., 2010).

<u>Mixed States</u>

In mixed states, there are symptoms of both depression and mania at the same time, either one of which can be more severe than the other. Sometimes mixed state periods can come and go during a single episode of illness. There is also considerable overlap with agitated depression. The mix of depression and impulsivity can be quite lethal in terms of suicide and violence.

Some people with bipolar disorder seem to be more prone to mixed states. Their illness is characterized by early onset, frequent episodes, substance abuse, often head trauma, and early severe stressors (Swann A., Goldberg J., 2007).

<u>Rapid Cycling</u>

This type exhibits frequently recurring (4+ episodes/yr) treatment resistant depression alternating with hypomanic/manic episodes. Rapid cycling is most commonly seen in female clients and with bipolar II disorder. It occurs in 15-25% of clients. Early onset is common. It is believed that antidepressants can initiate rapid cycling if they are used long-term. Variations include ultra-rapid (1 day to 1 week), ultradian (<24 hours), and continuous (Altman L., et al., 2004). Current research suggests that these distinctions are increasingly arbitrary (Schneck C., 2011).

The Manic Phase

Three stages of mania:
1) hypomania - energetic, extroverted, assertive, hypersexual, self-confident, rapid speech
2) mania - loss of judgment, euphoria, grandiose, paranoid, irritable, hyperactive, ideas of reference, pressured, manipulative, demanding, hyper-religious
3) psychotic - paranoid, hyperactive, assaultive, delusional, labile, depressed, circumstantial, distractible, confused. Delusions are the most frequent psychotic symptoms in mania. Hallucinations are less common. No symptom or cluster of symptoms reliably distinguishes bipolar mania from schizophrenia.

Diagnosing a history of mania is complicated by the fact that many patients do not remember their hypomania episodes as illnesses. A good social history, as well as talking with family members, is crucial.

Sleep Disruption

Decreased need for sleep is one of the criteria for mania and the ability to maintain energy without sufficient sleep is not seen in other disorders. Sleep disturbance usually escalates just before an episode, and it is the most common prodrome to mania. An increase is sleep is often associated with the onset of depression. Moderating sleep and social rhythms is often key to preventing relapse (Frank E., et al., 2006, 2008).

Medical Causes of Mania
<u>Drugs</u>: amphetamines, alprazolam, antidepressants, baclofen, bromide, bronchodilators, calcium, cocaine, corticosteroids, cyclobenzaprine, cyclosporine, decongestants, digitalis, flutamide, isoniazid, levodopa, methylphenidate, metoclopromide, Niridazole, phenocyclidine, procarbazine, procyclidine, Reserpine withdrawal, thyroid, tolmetin, antidepressants
<u>CNS disorders</u>: brain tumors, cerebrovascular disorder, trauma, epilepsy, Huntington's, multiple sclerosis, Pick's, postencephalitic, Parkinson's, spinocerebellar atrophy, Wilson's Disease
<u>Toxic/ Metabolic</u>: AIDS, calcium, Cushing's, hemodialysis, hyperthyroidism, influenza, neurosyphilis, postoperative, post St. Louis type A encephalitis, Q fever, lupus, vitamin B12 deficiency

Bipolar Depression
Depression is usually the first, and most frequent episode in bipolar illness, and most of the psychosocial impairment of bipolar disorder is due to depression. Compared with those whose first episode was mania, patients with a depressive onset have a more unstable course, more mixed states, and more suicidal behavior. This may be due in part to early treatment with antidepressants, which make bipolar disorder worse. Or it may reflect a more severe form of the illness.

Of great clinical interest is whether we can predict which depressions will convert to bipolar disorder. Approximately 20% of people originally diagnosed with major depression will have a manic episode. At this point, there are no markers, symptoms, or patient factors that makes such an identification possible (Schneck C., 2011).

Gender Issues
There is no gender difference in the incidence of bipolar I disorder. Both genders have onset in puberty, although men may have a slightly earlier onset. There is some evidence that women may have a more depressive course than men, who in turn may have more manic symptoms. Women have more comorbidities (anxiety, obesity, migraine, thyroid), greater relative increase in AODA and suicide, more rapid

cycling and mixed states (Suppes T., 2006). Women are more likely to be treated than men and receive treatment earlier in the illness (NESARC).

Polycystic ovary syndrome (PCOS) is a metabolic condition that occurs in 7-15% of reproductive-aged women. These women have elevated androgens, chronic anovulation, insulin resistance, elevated LDL's with low HDL's, and a 3x risk of endometrial cancer. (They do not necessarily have polycystic ovaries.) Women with epilepsy and women with bipolar disorder have a high risk of anovulatory disorders and PCOS. The mood stabilizer Valproate is also associated with PCOS (Rasgon N., 2006).

<u>Pregnancy</u>

Although 50% of women with bipolar disorder have the onset of symptoms within 1 year of menarche, many are not accurately diagnosed until they have had a child and developed postpartum depression (Swann 2004). The postpartum period is a high-risk period for women with bipolar disorder for depression, manic, mixed, and psychotic episodes. Postpartum psychosis is a medical emergency (Ketter T., 2006). Stopping a mood stabilizer, particularly abruptly, during pregnancy carries a high risk for recurrence of the illness (Viguera A., et al., 2007).

No psychotropic drugs are known to be safe for pregnancy or breastfeeding, but bipolar disorder itself is also dangerous for pregnancy due to substance abuse, poor self-care and suicide. When prescribing medication for bipolar reproductive-age females, it is important to remember that 50% of pregnancies in the U.S. are unplanned. Different drugs are associated with different risks, including birth defects. Valproate should not be considered a drug of first choice for women of reproductive age, especially if they are not on birth control, due to the high rate of birth defects (Morrell M., 2006).

Bipolar Disorder in Young People

Children and adolescents are being diagnosed with bipolar disorder in increasing numbers. From 1996 to 2004, the number of children diagnosed with bipolar disorder has increased by a factor of 6 from 1.3 to 7.3 per 100,000 (Blader J., Carlson G., 2007). The question is whether this represents an over-diagnosis of the condition. Currently, there is little agreement on the validity of symptoms such as elated mood and grandiosity in children, the role of irritability, whether symptoms must be episodic, or how to consider subthreshold presentations (Horst R., 2009). Nonetheless, the clinical consensus is that bipolar disorder is over-diagnosed in youth.

Classically, bipolar symptoms in children follow a cyclic pattern and are as follows:

> Mania: hyperactivity, irritability, psychosis/grandiosity, elated/expansive mood, rapid speech/racing thoughts, lack of need for sleep
>
> Depression: personality change, drop in grades, morbid/suicidal, pessimistic, somatic

A young person meeting these criteria would be said to fit the "narrow phenotype." They would be highly likely to be genetically related to another person with bipolar disorder. They will be likely to continue to have bipolar disorder symptoms as an adult. There is little controversy about this group among clinicians.

Some child psychiatrists believe that chronic severe irritability accompanied by aggression and volatility is the predominant mood state in children with bipolar disorder. Grandiosity and expansive mood need not be present. This is called the "broad phenotype." There is little evidence that this group will continue to be bipolar as adults. Furthermore, irritability is a very non-specific finding. In children, it is seen in oppositional defiant and conduct disorders, depression, anxiety, ADHD, autism, and PTSD. Most researchers consider irritability alone, no matter how extreme, to be inadequate in making a diagnosis of mania in youth (Horst R., 2009).

A second issue concerns how episodic the mood shifts should be. In adults, it is expected that there be clear inter-episode periods of recovery. Child psychiatrists, however, have described children with bipolar disorder who present with chronic, continuous rapid cycling, with low rates of inter-episode remission. Children have also been described with ultrarapid cycling, sometimes with multiple episodes in a day. At this point, however, an episodic course continues to be a reasonable requirement for increasing the probability of an accurate diagnosis (Horst R., 2009). This is confirmed by the Course and Outcome of Bipolar Youth (COBY) study of 413 youths with bipolar spectrum disorder. These young people had episodic illness with depressive and mixed symptoms with rapid mood changes (Brimaher B., et al., 2009).

Some researchers suggest a new category – severe mood dysregulation – to categorize children with chronic presentation, no discernable episodes, sometimes overlapping ADHD symptoms, and severe rage attacks. These children look very much like a combination of ADHD and oppositional defiant disorder (Brotman M., et al., 2007). The *DSM-5*® workgroup has proposed a similar disorder under Depression – Disruptive Mood Dysregulation Disorder – to try to capture the distinction of children who have rages but not mania.

A further complication of diagnosis is that up to 80% of children with bipolar disorder will also have ADHD. Distinguishing between the two is difficult. Grandiosity, elated mood, hypersexuality in the absence of sexual abuse, flight of ideas, decreased need for sleep, and episodic presentation seem to distinguish between bipolar disorder and ADHD (Horst R., 2009).

<u>Treatment</u>

Treatment should involve both psychotherapeutic and psychopharmacologic interventions. Family therapy with an emphasis on education and managing symptoms and treatment adherence is crucial. Studies regarding efficacy of medication in young people are very limited.

For ADHD, stimulants remain the treatment of choice. There is also evidence that stimulants may benefit some children with disruptive behavior disorders (oppositional defiant and conduct disorder) and bipolar disorder (Carlson G., 2009). The only medications approved for bipolar disorder in young people at this point are lithium (12 and up), and several second-generation antipsychotics for manic states (10-17.) Probably all of the atypical antipsychotics are effective for mania, but all cause significant weight gain. None of the anticonvulsants are useful (Gelenberg 2009, *Harvard Mental Health Letter,* 2009).

In summary, if the young person has classic symptoms of bipolar disorder, treat with a second generation antipsychotic. If they have severe ADHD with aggression (severe mood dysregulation, ADHD + a disruptive behavior disorder), treat with a stimulant, possibly adding risperidone (approved for treatment of irritability associated with pervasive developmental disorders.)

Genetics

Bipolar disorder is genetically linked. If one parent has bipolar illness, chances are 1:7 that their child will. Despite this clear genetic relationship, there are relatively few studies of the heritability of bipolar disorder. Part of the problem lies in the numerous subtypes of the disorder, and part of the problem is the categorical distinction between major depression and bipolar disorder (the presence of one manic episode) that confounds all genetic studies of depression since the disorders seem to be clearly related at some level. One study estimates heritability at 73%. Because the same study came up with a similar estimate for unipolar depression, the question arose as to whether the genetic vulnerability represented the same disease, with bipolar disorder being a more severe variant of major depression. If this is the case, what determines the development of bipolar vs. unipolar illness? There is no current research that answers this question, although it is fairly well established that non-shared environmental effects are more important than family environment (Jang K., 2005).

Comorbidity with Substance Abuse
Bipolar disorder is the affective disorder most commonly associated with substance abuse. 23.6% of bipolar clients have an alcohol use disorder, 12.9% have a drug abuse disorder, and 37% have nicotine dependence (NESARC).

Odds ratio of substance abuse in bipolar disorder (NESARC):

Substance	BPI	BPII
Alcohol abuse	3	3.9
Alcohol dependence	5.5	3.1
Drug abuse	5.9	3.9
Drug dependence	11.1	3.7

Bipolar clients are unreliable reporters of substance use. They also underreport psychiatric symptoms. Substance abuse complicates bipolar disorder and its diagnosis (Vornik L., Brown S., 2006).
1) Stimulants may precipitate a manic episode. Chronic use of CNS stimulants like amphetamine and cocaine cause euphoria, decreased appetite, increased energy, grandiosity, and sometimes paranoia that mimics mania
2) Treatment adherence declines with more frequent hospitalizations and lower rates of recovery
3) Patients report a lower quality of life than those who do not abuse substances

4) Substance abuse is related to higher mortality by suicide (15-19%) and other causes

Treatment of one does not resolve the other, but controlled bipolar disease usually leads to the diminishing of substance abuse symptoms.

Natural History of Bipolar Disorder

Onset can occur at any time, from childhood to old age, but most commonly in adolescence. Early onset of depression, anxiety disorder, substance abuse, and behavioral disorders are all linked to eventual diagnosis of bipolar disorder in those with a family history of bipolar disorder. (Swann A., Goldberg J., 2007).

30% of bipolar clients have both manic and depressive episodes, 32% have mixed manic and depression, 22% have only manic episodes, and 10% have only mixed episodes. Depression is the most frequent episode. Depressive episodes last longer (25.4 weeks) than manic episodes (5.5 weeks). 48.5% of bipolar clients will have an anxiety disorder and 70.8% will have a personality disorder (NESARC).

Severe psychosocial stressors appear more important in the first episode than latter episodes - each episode requires less stress to occur. 90% of clients who have one manic episode will have another. Two years after remission, even with excellent treatment 49% will have relapsed. The interval between episodes will usually diminish and episodes will become more treatment resistant (Perlis R., 2006).

Since 1990, there is evidence that clinicians are seeing more cycling, mixed states, and lithium resistance. Age of onset seems to be declining and there is increased prevalence in younger people. This corresponds with a 10x increase in prescriptions for antidepressants (Ghaemi S., 2008).

Bipolar disorder is associated with high morbidity and mortality. Medical problems associated with bipolar disorder include cardiovascular disease, diabetes, obesity and thyroid disease. In addition, risk factors associated with nicotine use, alcohol and drug abuse, anxiety and eating disorders lead to early onset of medical diseases (Roshanaei-Moghaddam B., Katon W., 2009).

Diagnosis

A recent review of 85 sequential admissions to a dual diagnosis unit who were diagnosed with bipolar disorder and substance abuse found that 67% were misdiagnosed as bipolar. The misdiagnosis occurred because clinicians were confused by the mood instability caused by substance abuse, and failed to carefully evaluate for the presence of clear manic episodes when the patients were abstinent (Goldberg J., et al., 2008).

Because of the importance of identifying bipolar disorder correctly and therefore, not exposing the patient to ineffective or dangerous therapy (e.g. antidepressants), it is important to do a careful evaluation looking for the presence of manic episodes, and a cyclic pattern in the illness. A life chart is a good way to do this. Life chart templates are available on the web at NIMH. Also, consider non-manic markers of the illness. These include (Phelps J., 2007):

- Family history of mood and substance abuse problems
- Early age of onset
- Illness course over time
- Poor response to antidepressants in the past

Treatment

The prevention of episodes improves long-term prognosis. The Systematic Treatment Enhancement Program for Bipolar Disorder (STEP-BD) is a 7-year NIMH study with 4,361 participants at 20 sites to provide optimum treatment (Perlis, 2006). The early findings from STEP-BD indicate that with state-of-the-art care, 58.4% of clients will achieve recovery, but 5% of clients will relapse each month, 48.5% within 2 years, and that 80% of the relapses will be to depression. One of the strongest predictors of relapse is residual symptoms. There is no evidence that antidepressants improve recovery, either with or without mood stabilizers.

Trying to determine the best treatment for bipolar disorder is one of the most complex clinical challenges in psychiatry. Every month brings new information, often of questionable usefulness. The difficulty so far has been that the three aspects of bipolar disorder – mania, depression, and relapse – all seem to respond differently to different treatments. The following is a general summary based on a synthesis of many trials (Carey T., et al., 2008, Schneck C., et al., 2008, Goldberg J., et al., 2007):

<u>Mania and relapse of mania (first 3 months after treatment for mania)</u>

Lithium remains the gold standard for the treatment of mania. It has a large research base and also has suicide prevention effects. It is less effective in mixed mania and rapid cycling. It may work better early in the illness and may lose effectiveness if it is stopped and restarted several times. It does not work as well when there is comorbid substance abuse.

The first and second-generation antipsychotics all treat manic episodes. First generation antipsychotics may cause depression.

The anticonvulsants divalproex and carbamazepine are effective, as is electroconvulsive therapy. There is no good evidence of manic response to topiramate, gabapentin, lamotrigine, or oxcarbazepine, although lamotrigine may be helpful for mixed episodes.

Bipolar depression and relapse of depression (first 3 months after treatment)

The newer antidepressants cause switching into mania from a depressive episode about 20-30% of the time. This is half the rate of switching caused by older antidepressants (TCA's, MAOI's.) If there is also treatment by a mood stabilizer, switching rates are reduced further. Bipolar II patients switch to hypomania half as frequently as bipolar I patients switch to mania. STEP-BD does not recommend using antidepressants at all. Some other studies do, if there is concomitant use of a mood stabilizer.

Lithium, lamotrigine, quetiapine, and olanzapine (and olanzapine+fluoxetine) have been shown to have some efficacy in treating bipolar depression. All other medications are either unproven or ineffective.

Maintenance (1 year after episode)

The most robust evidence is for lithium, olanzapine for the prevention of mania, and aripiprazole for the prevention of mania.

Carbamazepine, valproate, and lamotrigine each have a few studies showing efficacy in maintenance, but the quality of the evidence is low. There seems to be little reason to choose one over any of the others. Efficacy for bipolar II disorder is uncertain. There is some suggestion that the calcium channel blocker verapamil and omega-3 fatty acids may be alternative treatments for prohylaxis during pregnancy.

There is fairly strong evidence that long-term treatment with antidepressants not only does not protect from further depressive episodes, but also destabilize the illness, even in the presence of a mood stabilizer. Antidepressants, if used at all, should only be used short term.

Most people with bipolar disorder end up taking at least two medications for their illness, and we know very little about using combinations of drugs.

Non-Pharmaceutical Interventions

Cognitive behavioral therapy and psychoeducation have been shown to prevent relapse. Certain common principles can be described (Roman B., Gillig P., 2006, Frank E., et al., 2006):

1) Identify signs of relapse and make plans for an early response
2) Use education to increase the likelihood of adherence
3) Practice stress management and problem solving
4) Maintain regular rhythms for exercise, sleep and eating
5) Keep negative expressed emotion in the family at a minimum
6) Don't make important decisions while symptomatic

A review of these various strategies indicates that early recognition of mood symptoms and treatment adherence have the strongest effect in preventing manic relapse. Cognitive and interpersonal coping strategies have the strongest effect on preventing depressive relapse (Miklowitz D., 2008).

Treatment Adherence

Rates of non-adherence to treatment for bipolar disorder range from non-adherent (21.4%) to partially adherent (24.5%) in one large VA study (Sajatovic M., et al., 2007). People with bipolar disorder often have limited insight. This isn't denial or wish to distort the facts. There is something in the illness that distorts the way they see themselves and the world. Regardless of the reason, the best predictor of a poor outcome is poor treatment adherence.

BIBLIOGRAPHY

Altman L, et al. Bipolar Moving Target. *Current Psych* (Nov 2004) 3:11;13-22.

Anthenelli R. How and Why to Help Psychiatric Patients Stop Smoking. *Curr Psych* (Jan 2006) 4:1;77-87.

Artaloytia J, et al. Negative Signs and Symptoms Secondary to Antipsychotics: A Double-Blind, Randomized Trial of a Single Dose of Placebo, Haloperidol, and Risperidone in Healthy Volunteers. *Am J Psych* (March 2006) 163:488-493.

Baldessarini R. Reducing Suicide Risk in Psychiatric Disorders. *Curr Psychiatry* (Sept 2003) Vol 2(9), 14-24.

Birmaher B, et al. Four-Year Longitudinal Course of Children and Adolescents With Bipolar Spectrum Disorders: The Course and Outcome of Bipolar Youth (COBY) Study. *Am J Psych* (July 2009) 166:7;795-804.

Blader J, Carlson G. Increased Rates of Bipolar Diagnoses Among U.S. Child, Adolescent, and Adult Inpatients. 1996-2004. *Biol Psych* (2007) 62:107-114.

Brotman M, et al. Parental Diagnoses in Youth With Narrow Phenotype Bipolar Disorder or Severe Mood Dysregulation. *Am J Psych* (Aug 2007) 164:8; 1238-1241.

Brown A, Derkits E. Prenatal Infection and Schizophrenia: A Review of Epidemiologic and Translational Studies. *Am J Psych* (March 2010) 167:3;261-280.

Buckley P. Prevalence and Consequences of the Dual Diagnosis of Substance Abuse and Severe Mental Illness. *J Clin Psych* (2006) 67(suppl 7) 5-9.

Carey T, et al. Extracting Key Messages from Systematic Reviews. *J Psych Pract* (March 2008) 14 (suppl 1) 28-34.

Carlat D. Light Therapy for Depression: Does It Work? *Carlat Psych Rep* (Oct 2006) 4:10.

Carlat D. How Do STAR-D Results Help Our Depressed Patients? *Carlat Psych Rep* (Jan 2007) 1-8.

Carlson G. Treating the Childhood Bipolar Controversy: A Tale of Two Children. *Am J Psych* (Jan 2009) 166:1;18-24.

Carney R, Freedland K. Treatment Resistant Depression and Mortality After Acute Coronary Syndrome. *Am J Psych* (April 2009) 166:4;410-417.

Carpenter W. Conceptualizing Schizophrenia Through Attenuated Symptoms in the Population. *Am J Psych* (Sept 2010) 167:9;1013-1016.

Clark R, Samnaliev M. Psychosocial Treatment in the 21st Century. *Intl J Law Psych* (2005) 28:532-544.

Cohen C, et al. Outcome Among Community Dwelling Older Adults With Schizophrenia: Results Using Five Conceptual Models. *Comm Ment Health J* (April 2008) 45:2;151-156.

Cohen L, et al. Risk for New Onset of Depression During the Menopausal Transition. *Arch Gen Psych* (Apr 2006) 63:385-390.

Cuijpers P, et al. Adding Psychotherapy to Pharmacotherapy in the Treatment of Depressive Disorders in Adults: A Meta-Analysis. *J Clin Psych* (Sept 2009) 70:9;1219-1229.

Daumit G, et al. Adverse Events During Medical and Surgical Hospitalizations for Persons With Schizophrenia. *Arch Gen Psych* (March 2006) 63:267-272.

de Jonge P, et al. Nonresponse to Treatment for Depression Following Myocardial Infarction: Association With Subsequent Cardiac Events. *Am J Psych* (Sept 2007) 164:9; 1371-1378.

Dickerson F, et al. Evidence-Based Psychotherapy for Schizophrenia. *J Nerv Ment Dis* (Jan 2006) 194:1; 3-9.

Dominguez M, et al. Early Expression of Negative/Disorganized Symptoms Predicting Psychotic Experiences and Subsequent Clinical Psychosis: A 10-Year Study. *Am J Psych* (Sept 2010) 167:9;1075-1082.

Drake R, et al. Ten-Year Recovery Outcomes for Clients With Co-Occurring Schizophrenia and Substance Use Disorders. *Schiz Bull* (March 2006) 32:3;464-473.

Eaton W, et al. Association of Schizophrenia and Autoimmune Diseases: Linkage of Danish National Registers. *Am J Psych* (March 2006) 163:3; 521-528.

Emslie G. Improving Outcome in Pediatric Depression. *Am J Psych* (Jan 2008)165:1;1-3.

Evins A, et al. Schizophrenia: More Than Classical Symptoms. *Clin Psych News Suppl* (2004)

Fazel S, et al. Risk Factors for Violent Crime in Schizophrenia: A National Cohort Study of 13,806 Patients. *J Clin Psych* (March 2009) 70:3;362-369.

Flynn H. Epidemiology and Phenomenology of Postpartum Mood Disorders. *Psych Ann* (July 2005) 35:7;544-551.

Foti, D et al. Cannabis Use and the Course of Schizophrenia: 10-Year Follow-up After First Hospitalization. *Am J Psych* (2010)167-987-993.

Frank E, et al. The Importance of Routine for Preventing Recurrence in Bipolar Disorder. *Am J Psych* (June 2006) 163:6; 981-985.

Frank E. et al. The Roles of Interpersonal and Social Rhythm Therapy in Improving Occupational Functioning in Patients with Bipolar I Disorder. *Am J Psych* (Dec 2008) 165:12;1559-1565.

Fu C, et al. Neural Responses to Happy Facial Expressions in Major Depression Following Antidepressant Treatment. *Am J Psych* (April 2007) 164:599-607.

Gaschler K. Misery in Motherhood. *Sci Am Mind* (Feb/Mar 2008) 67-73.

Gelenberg A. Divalproex for Mania in Children and Adolescents: A Negative Study. *Bio Ther Psych* (Oct 2009) 32:10;1.

Geppert C, Minkoff K. Issues in Dual Diagnosis: Diagnosis, Treatment, and New Research. *Psych Times*. (April 2004) 103-107.

Ghaemi S. Treatment of Rapid Cycling Disorder: Are Antidepressants Mood Stabilizers? *Am J Psych* (March 2008) 165:3;300-302.

Gillespie C, et al. Early Life Stress and Depression. *Current Psych* (Oct 2005) 4:10; 15-30.

Gilmore J. Understanding What Causes Schizophrenia: A Developmental Perspective. *Am J Psych* (Jan 2010) 1687:1;8-10.

Gladstone T, et al. The Prevention of Adolescent Depression. *Psych Clin N Am* (2010) 34:35-52.

Goldberg J, et al. Overdiagnosis of Bipolar Disorder Among Substance Use Disorder Inpatients With Mood Instability. *J Clin Psych* (Nov 2008) 69:1;1751-1757.

Goldberg J. et al. Adjunctive Antidepressant Use and Symptomatic Recovery Among Bipolar Depressed Patients With Concomitant Manic Symptoms: Findings From the STEP-BD. *Am J Psych* (Sept 2007) 164:9;1348-1355.

Gray M, et al. Crisis Debriefing: What Helps and What Might Not. *Curr Psych* (2006)5:10;17-29.

Green A, et al. Schizophrenia and Co-occurring Substance Use Disorder. *Am J Psych* (March 2007) 164:3; 402-408.

Green M. Cognition, Drug Treatment, and Functional Outcome in Schizophrenia: A Tale of Two Transitions. *Am J Psych* (July 2007) 164:7; 992-994.

Hallfors D, et al. Which Comes First in Adolescence-Sex and Drugs or Depression? *Am J Prev Med* (2005) 29:3; 163-170.

Harrow M, et al. Do Patients With Schizophrenia Ever Show Periods of Recovery? A 15-Year Multi-Follow-Up Study. *Schiz Bull* (July 2005) 31:3; 723-734.

Hasin D, et al. Epidemiology of Major Depressive Disorder. *Arch Gen Psych* (Oct 2005) 62;1097-1106.

Henquet C, et al. The Environment and Schizophrenia: The Role of Cannabis Use. *Schiz Bull* (June 2005) 31:3;608-612.

Hensley P. A Review of Bereavement-Related Depression and Complicated Grief. *Psych Ann* (Sept 2006) 36:9;619-626.

Hofer A, et al. Quality of Life in Schizophrenia: The Impact of Psychopathology, Attitude Toward Medication, and Side Effects. *J Clin Psych* (July 2004) 65:932-939.

Hollon S, et al. Treatment and Prevention of Depression. *Psych Sci Pub Int* (Nov 2002) 3:2;39-77.

Holzheimer III P, Mayfield H. Deep Brain Stimulation for Treatment-Resistant Depression. *Am J Psych* (Dec 2010) 167:12;1437-1444

Horst R. Diagnostic Issues in Bipolar Disorder. *Psych Clin N Am* (2009) 32:71-80.

Jamison K. Suicide and Bipolar Disorder. *J Clin Psych* (2000) 61 (Suppl 9) 47-51.

Jang K. *The Behavioral Genetics of Psychopathology: A Clinical Guide.* (2005) New Jersey: Lawrence Earlbaum Assoc. Inc.

Johnson P, Flake E. Maternal Depression and Child Outcomes. *Psych Ann* (2007) 37:6;404-410.

Kendler K, et al. Sex Differences in the Relationship Between Social Support and Risk for Major Depression: A Longitudinal Study of Opposite-Sex Twin Pairs. *Am J Psych* (2005)162:2; 250-256

Kendler K, et al. A Swedish National Twin Study of Lifetime Major Depression. *Am J Psych* (2006) 163:109-114.

Kessler R, et al. Lifetime and 12-Month Prevalence of DSM-III-R Psychiatric Disorders in the United States: Results from the National Comorbidity Survey. *Arch Gen Psych* (1994) 51:8-19.

Kessler R, et al. Prevalence and Effects of Mood Disorders on Work Performance in a Nationally Representative Sample of U.S. Workers. *Am J Psych* (Sept 2006) 163:9; 1561-1568.

Kessler R, et al. Prevalence, Severity, and Comorbidity of 12-Month *DSM-IV* Disorders in the National Comorbidity Survey Replication. *Arch Gen Psych* (Jun 2005) 62:617-627.

Ketter T. Effects of the Female Reproductive System on Bipolar Disorder. *CNS Spect* (May 2006) 11:5; (Suppl 5) 5-6.

Khurana A, et al. Childhood-Onset Schizophrenia: Diagnostic and Treatment Challenges. *Psych Times* (Feb 2007) 33-36.

Krabbendam L, Os J. Schizophrenia and Urbanicity: A Major Environmental Influence-Conditional on Genetic Risk. *Schiz Bull* (Sep 2005) 31:4; 795-799.

Krishnan V, Nestler E. Linking Molecules to Mood: New Insight Into the Biology of Depression. *Am J Psych* (Nov 2010) 167:11;1305-1320.

Kuipers E. Psychological Therapies for Schizophrenia: Family and Cognitive Interventions. *Psych Times* (Feb 2007) 36-40.

Lieberman J, Stroup T. NIMH-CATIE Schizophrenia Study: What Did We Learn? *Am J Psych* (Aug 2011) 168:8;770-775.

Lieberman J, et al. Preventing Clinical Deterioration in the Course of Schizophrenia: The Potential for Neuroprotection. *CNS Spect* (April 2006) 11:4; (Suppl 4) 1-13.

Luby J. Early Childhood Depression. *Am J Psych* (Sept 2009) 166:9;974-979.

MacDonald A, Schulz S. What We Know: Findings That Every Theory of Schizophrenia Should Explain. *Schiz Bull* (2009) 35:3;493-508.

Magnusson A, Partonen T. The Diagnosis, Symptomatology, and Epidemiology of Seasonal Affective Disorder. *CNS Spect* (2005) 10:8;625-634.

Marder S, et al. Physical Health Monitoring of Patients with Schizophrenia. *Am J of Psych* (Aug 2004) 161:8; 1334-1349.

Mayberg, H. Defining Neurocircuits in Depression. *Psych Ann* (April 2006) 36:4;259-268.

McNiel DE, et al. The Relationship Between Command Hallucinations and Violence. *Psych Serv* (2000) 51:1288-1292.

Meyer J. The Metabolic Syndrome and Schizophrenia: Clinical Research Update. *Psych Times* (Feb 2007) 29-32.

Miklowitz D. Adjunctive Psychotherapy for Bipolar Disorder: State of the Evidence. *Am J Psych* (Nov 2008) 165:11;1408-1419.

Morrell M. Effects of *In Utero* Exposure to AED's on Morphology and Neurodevelopment. *CNS Spect* (May 2006) 11:5; (Suppl 5) 9-10.

Nonacs R, Cohen L. Assessment and Treatment of Depression During Pregnancy: an Update. *Psych Clin of N Am* (2003) 26;547-562.

Ongur, D. Topics in the Treatment of Schizophrenia. *Carlat Psych Rep* (Dec 2009) 4-5.

Palmer B et al. The Lifetime Risk of Suicide in Schizophrenia. *Arch Gen Psychiatry* (Mar 2005) 62:247-253.

Paris J. Personality Disorders and Mood Disorders: Phenomenological Resemblances vs. Pathogenetic Pathways. *J Pers Dis* (2010) 24:1;3-13.

Parker, G, et al. Timing is Everything: The Onset of Depression and Acute Coronary Syndrome Outcome. *Bio Psych* (Oct15, 2008) 64:8

Parry P. A Commentary on "Editor's Perspective: Do Antidepressants Work in Kids?" *Carlat Child Psych Report* (Oct 2010).

Perlis R, et al. Predictors of Recurrence in Bipolar Disorder: Primary Outcomes from the Systematic Treatment Enhancement Program for Bipolar Disorder (STEP-BD). *Am J Psych* (2006) 63:217-224.

Phelps J. Bipolar Diagnosis: Navigating Between Scylla and Charybdis. *Psych Times* (May 2007) 20-23.

Pies R. Prenatal Antidepressant Use: Time for a Pregnant Pause? *Psych Times* (Sept 2006) 69-71.

Pies R. Beyond Reliability: Biomarkers and Validity in Psychiatry. *Psych 2008* (Jan 2008) 48-52.

Potter G, Steffens D. Depression and Cognitive Impairment in Older Adults. *Psych Times* (Nov 2007) 23-30.

Quitkin FM, et al. Remission Rates with 3 Consecutive Antidepressant Trials: Effectiveness for Depressed Outpatients. *J Clin Psych* (2005) 66:670-676.

Rasgon N. Selection of Appropriate Therapy: Valproate and Reproductive Function. *CNS Spect* (May 2006) 11:5; (Suppl 5) 7-8.

Ray W, et al. Atypical Antipsychotic Drugs and the Risk of Sudden Cardiac Death. *NEJM* (Jan 15, 2009) 360:3;225-235.

Reiss D. Transmission and Treatment of Depression. *Am J Psych* (Sept 2008) 165:9;1083-1085.

Roman B, et al. More Than Medication. *Psychiatry 2006* (March) 56-61.

Rosenheck R. Barriers to Employment for People With Schizophrenia. *Am J Psych* (March 2006) 163:411-417.

Roshanaei-Moghaddam B, Katon W. Premature Mortality From General Medical Illnesses Among Personal With Bipolar Disorder: A Review. *Psych Serv* (Feb 2009) 60:2;147-156.

Sabb F, Bilder R. Schizophrenia: From Bench to Bedside: The Future of Neuroimaging Tools in Diagnosis and Treatment. *Psych Times* (Feb 2006) 33-48.

Saha S, et al. A Systematic Review of Mortality in Schizophrenia. *Arch Gen Psych* (Oct 2007) 64:10; 1123-1131.

Sajatovic M, et al. Treatment Adherence With Lithium and Anticonvulsant Medications Among Patients With Bipolar Disorder. *Psych Serv* (June 2007) 58:6; 855-863.

Saran M et al. Biological Markers and the Future of Early Diagnosis and Treatment in Schizophrenia *Psych Times* (Feb 2007) 19-21.

Schneck C. Bipolar Phenomenology: Have We Learned All We Can Learn? *Am J Psych* (Jan 2011) 168:1;4-6.

Schneck C, et al. The Prospective Course of Rapid-Cycling Bipolar Disorder: Findings From the STEP-BD. *Am J Psych* (March 2008) 165:3;370-377.

Schneider F, et al. Impairment in the Specificity of Emotion Processing in Schizophrenia. *Am J Psych* (March 2006) 163:442-447.

Seeman M. Gender Issues in Psychiatry. *Focus* (Winter 2006) 4:1; 3-5.

Seeman M. Gender Differences in the Prescribing of Antipsychotic Drugs *Am J of Psych* (August 2004) 161:8; 1324-1333.

Sergi M, et al. Social Perception as a Mediator of the Influence of Early Visual Processing on Functional Status in Schizophrenia. *Am J Psych* (March 2006) 163:448-454.

Shear K. Bereavement Related Depression in the Elderly. *CNS Spect* (Aug 2005) 10:8; Suppl 8;3-5.

Shear K. Grief and Depression: Treatment Decisions for Bereaved Children and Adults. *Am J Psych* (July 2009) 166:7;746-748.

Shelton R. Depression: The Role of Inflammation in the Body. *NAMI Advocate* (Winter 2012) 14-17.

Silk K. The Quality of Depression in Borderline Personality Disorder and the Diagnostic Process. *J Pers Dis* (2010) 24:1;25-37.

Simon G, Perlis R. Personalized Medicine for Depression: Can We Match Patients with Treatments? *Am J Psych* (Dec 2010) 167:12;1445-1455.

Singh M, et al. Pharmacotherapy for Child and Adolescent Mood Disorders. *Psych Ann* (July 2007) 37:7; 465-476.

Sloan D, Kornstein S. Gender Difference in Depression and Response to Antidepressant Treatment. *Psych Clin N Am* (2003) 26;581-94.

Suppes T. Gender Differences in Bipolar Disorder. *CNS Spect* (May 2006) 11:5; (Suppl 5) 2-4.

Suri R, et al. Effects of Antenatal Depression and Antidepressant Treatment on Gestational Age at Birth and Risk of Preterm Birth. *Am J Psych* (Aug 2007) 164:1206-1213.

Swann A. Special Needs of Women With Bipolar Disorder. *Symposium Monograph Suppl* (Aug 2004) 3-10.

Swann A, Goldberg J. Assessing the Bipolar Spectrum and Improving Outcomes. *Reporter* (Suppl *Psych Times*) (Ap 2007) 1-7.

Swartz M, et al. Substance Use and Psychosocial Functioning in Schizophrenia Among New Enrollees in the NIMH CATIE Study. *Psych Serv* (Aug 2006) 57:8; 1110-1116.

Tenhula W, et al. Behavioral Treatment of Substance Abuse in Schizophrenia. *J Clin Psych: In Sess* (2009) 65:8;831-841.

Terman M, Terman J. Light Therapy for Seasonal and Nonseasonal Depression: Efficacy, Protocol, Safety, and Side Effects. *CNS Spect* (Aug 2005) 10:8;647-662.

Thraenhardt B. Hearing Voices. *Sci Am Mind* (Dec 2006/Jan 2007) 74-77.

Trivedi MH, et al. Evaluation of Outcomes with Citalopram for Depression Using Measurement-Based Care in STAR*D: Implications for Clinical Practice. *Am J Psych* (2006) 163:28-40.

Tully E, et al. An Adoption Study of Parental Depression as an Environmental Liability for Adolescent Depression and Childhood Disruptive Disorders. *Am J Psych* (Sept 2008) 165:9;1148-1154.

Turkington D, et al. Cognitive Behavior for Schizophrenia. *Am J Psych* (March 2006) 163:365-373.

Van Rhoads R, Gelenberg A. Treating Depression to Remission. *Curr Psych* (Sept 2005) 4:9; 14-28.

Viguera A, et al. Risk of Recurrence in Women With Bipolar Disorder During Pregnancy: Prospective Study of Mood Stabilizer Discontinuation. *Am J Psych* (Dec 2007) 164:12; 1817-1824.

Volavka J, Citrome L. Pathways to Aggression in Schizophrenia Affect Results of Treatment. *Schiz Bull* (2011) 37:5; 921-929.

Vornik L, Brown E. Management of Comorbid Bipolar Disorder and Substance Abuse. *J Clin Psych* (2006) 67: (Suppl 7) 24-30.

Walkup J. Treatment of Depressed Adolescents. *Am J Psych* (July 2010) 167:7;734-737.

Widom C, et al. A Prospective Investigation of Major Depressive Disorder and Comorbidity in Abused and Neglected Children Grown Up. *Arch Gen Psych* (2007) 64:49-56.